21ST
CENTURY
DEBATES

MEDIA

THE IMPACT ON OUR LIVES

JULIAN PETLEY

HODDER
Wayland

an imprint of Hodder Children's Books

21st Century Debates Series

Genetics	Surveillance	Climate Change	Energy
Internet	Media	Rainforests	Waste and Recycling

Produced for Hodder Wayland by Discovery Books Limited, Unit 3, 37 Watling Street, Leintwardine, Shropshire SY7 0LW, England

Published in Great Britain in 2000 by Hodder Wayland, an imprint of Hodder Children's Books

Editor: Patience Coster
Series editor: Alex Woolf
Series design: Mind's Eye Design, Lewes

With thanks to Lucy Perry-Smith at J Walter Thompson

A Catalogue record for this book is available from the British Library

ISBN 0 7502 2769 9

Printed and bound in Italy by G. Canale & C.S.p.A., Turin

Hodder Children's Books, a division of Hodder Headline Limited, 338 Euston Road, London NW1 3BH

Picture acknowledgements: AFP/Corbis 28; Aquarius Library 11; Aquarius Library/Warner Bros 43; BBC Television 19; Bettmann/Corbis 7, 8, 23, 41; Corbis 15 (David Turnley), 16 (Vittoriano Rastelli), 21 (Marc Garanger), 22 (Peter Turnley), 30, 32 (Lynn Goldsmith), 34 (Christine Gerstenberg), 35 (Paul A Souders), 39 (Laura Dwight), 50 (Marko Shark), 51 (Peter Turnley), 54 (Michael S Yamashita), 55 (Julie Houck), 58 (R W Jones), 59 (Mark Gibson); Corbis/Everett 6, 44; Hulton-Deutsch Collection/Corbis 4; Hulton Getty 5, 12, 13; Popperfoto 10, 40; Popperfoto/Reuters 14, 25, 31, 45, 46, 49, 52, 56; Reuters NewMedia Inc/Corbis 48; Ronald Grant Archive 17, 27, 42; Tesco 57; J Walter Thompson 37, 38.

Cover: foreground picture shows journalists jostling to photograph Princess Diana as she arrives in Lahore, India, in February 1996 (Popperfoto/Reuters); background picture shows advertising hoardings and banners in a busy street in Shanghai City, China (Tony Stone Images).

CONTENTS

WHAT ARE 'THE MEDIA'?

An Information Revolution – or Just More Technology?

The word 'media' is the plural of the word 'medium'. According to the *Concise Oxford Dictionary*, a medium is 'the means by which something is communicated'. In this sense, you use your voice as a medium when you speak to someone, and a school essay is a written medium for communicating your ideas and experiences.

However, when people talk about the media today, they're almost always referring to much larger and more technologically elaborate forms of communication. It is because these communications systems are capable of reaching such vast numbers of people – right across the globe in some cases – that they are sometimes called the 'mass media'.

A printing press from the sixteenth century. Printed books and pamphlets were the first media, but widespread illiteracy meant that, to begin with, these reached only the educated few.

The invention of printing

The story of the media really begins with the invention of printing in Europe at the end of the fifteenth century. At first, only small quantities of books were printed: not only was the printing technology extremely basic by modern standards but very few people could actually read. Almost everything that was printed was of a religious nature, and in Latin.

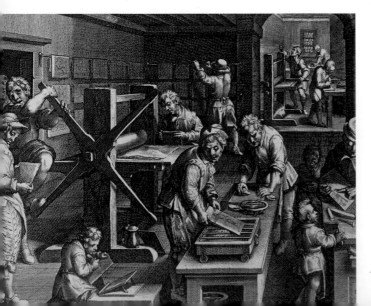

During the next century, however, printing became a minor industry, and a wider range of publications started to appear. It is from this point that the questions which we still associate with the media today began to be raised: who should be allowed to publish, what should they be allowed to publish, who should be allowed to regulate the contents of the media, and on what grounds should the regulators regulate? In many ways, the history of the printed media, certainly in Europe, is also the history of the media's attempt to escape from regulations imposed upon them by the authorities.

The popular press

By the 1880s, in Europe and America, the newspaper as we know it today, with its mix of news, comment and 'human interest' stories, its reliance on advertising, and its division into different formats, had already established itself. This was greatly aided by the spread of mass literacy. With the rise of the popular press there also came the attacks upon it, which still ring out to this day.

In 1887 the cultural critic Matthew Arnold argued that the new, popular journalism 'has much to recommend it; it is full of ability, novelty, variety, sensation, sympathy, generous instincts; its one great fault is that it is featherbrained'. Meanwhile, a cynical verse was circulating Fleet Street, the home of the British press:

'Tickle the public, make 'em grin,
The more you tickle, the more you'll win;
Teach the public, you'll never get rich,
You'll live like a beggar and die in a ditch.'

In other words, a newspaper will be much more successful financially if it merely entertains the public, as opposed to trying to educate them.

VIEWPOINTS

'A newspaper which glows with the colour of sunshine and throws light into dark places.'
Ella Wheeler Wilcox on the popular, 'yellow' press in The Worlds and I, *1919.*

'The rabble vomit their bile and call it a newspaper....'
The philosopher Friedrich Nietzsche in Thus Spake Zarathustra, *1883-5.*

The press baron, William Randolph Hearst, did not hesitate to use his popular newspapers such as the New York Journal *for propaganda purposes.*

Meanwhile, in the United States, popular newspapers that had been celebrated for discussing the issues of the day in a lively but nonetheless responsible manner began to be criticized. Dubbed the 'yellow press', they came under attack for their circulation-boosting stunts and sensationalism. The phrase 'yellow press' or 'yellow journalism' was coined at the end of the nineteenth century and was probably shortened from 'Yellow Kid journalism', which referred to the 'Yellow Kid', a 1895 cartoon in the *New York World*, a newspaper with a reputation for sensationalism. As the press historian and journalist Matthew Engel has put it, these nineteenth-century newspapers were 'cheap, ferociously competitive, rude, sensationalist, scurrilous and insulting' – similar, in fact, to the popular press today.

Cinema, radio and television
In the mid-1890s, an entirely new medium, cinema, came into being in Europe and the United States. Even before the end of the First World War, the American cinema had established the dominant position in the world market that it still enjoys. With the rise to prominence of Hollywood in the 1920s, and the establishment of film industries in countries such as France, Denmark and Germany, the movies came to be regarded as the new art form of the twentieth century. This process was given a tremendous boost at the end of the decade with the coming of sound.

But movies were not the only new form of communication. Commercial radio broadcasting began in the United States in 1920, with the National Broadcasting

Silent films such as Buster Keaton's The General *attracted huge audiences and contributed to the rise to prominence of Hollywood in the 1920s.*

Corporation (NBC) and the Columbia Broadcasting System (CBS) soon firmly established as rival giants, controlling stations across the country. On the other side of the Atlantic, the British Broadcasting Company, from which advertising was firmly barred, started its transmissions in 1922. By the end of the decade, radio had established itself as an extremely popular medium in many parts of the globe. Its dominance as a domestic medium was, however, to end with the coming of television.

By the mid-1950s television had become an established part of the furniture in the majority of American homes.

The first regular television transmissions took place in the 1930s in Britain and Germany, but Americans had to wait until the end of the decade to receive a comparable service. Nowhere before the Second World War could television be called a mass medium. Television sets were extremely expensive and signals could not be transmitted great distances, so television audiences were relatively small. It was only in the late 1940s in the United States and the mid-1950s in Europe that television actually took off – and then it did so with such spectacular success that for a time it looked as if it might actually eclipse the cinema.

FACT

In 1994 it was estimated that there were 80 televisions per 100 people in North America, but only 2.5 per 100 people in sub-Saharan Africa.

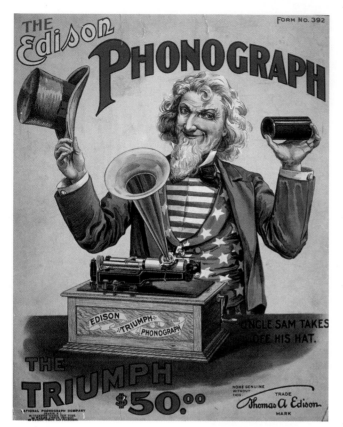

Uncle Sam doffs his hat to the Edison phonograph, an early form of gramophone invented in the United States by Thomas Edison in 1877.

Cinema, radio and television all make use of music, but we shouldn't forget that music has its very own media too. The gramophone was first developed in the United States in the 1880s, and by the 1920s the making of records and of various kinds of record players had become a major entertainment industry. Its obvious advantage over the radio was that listeners could hear the music they wanted when they wanted it. From the 1920s on, the music industry and equipment manufacturers were constantly developing new and more efficient ways of delivering music – from the long-playing record and the single, to the cassette and the compact disc.

Video and DVD

At the end of the 1970s another new medium appeared in our homes: video. Video recording had been around since the late 1950s, but the technology was rarely used outside the television studio. It wasn't until the early 1980s that the video recorder began to become a feature in an ever-increasing number of homes. The renting and selling of films on video became a lucrative business. And now the much more versatile DVD (a CD with images, text and music on it) looks set to replace the familiar videocassette.

Convergence

As the twentieth century neared its close, a whole series of developments began to rock the media scene and to change its face dramatically. These can best be summed up in the word 'convergence' – the coming together of the once separate broadcasting and telecommunications services. Put more simply, convergence means the union of the telephone, the television and the home computer.

All of this has been made possible by a number of developments. The mass production of microchips has made massive computer power available cheaply to the domestic consumer, whereas before the high cost of computer hard- and soft-ware had limited its use to large companies or state institutions. The laying of fibre-optic cables means that vast amounts of information can be carried at staggering speeds. For an increasing number of people, the most impressive pay-off of these developments has been access to the Internet – a vast collection of computer networks that use a common computer language and function as a single, virtual network. In Europe, the deregulation of (removing restrictions from) telecommunications and broadcasting has allowed new commercial players to enter the field. This means that the strict rules governing who can broadcast what have been considerably relaxed.

Finally, the development of digitalization means that every kind of information can be easily stored, readily manipulated and rapidly transmitted, all by computers. It is the fact that digitalization makes so much more information available to us so fast, and enables us to do so many things with it, that makes it such a crucial development of the modern media.

These, then, are the forms of media that go to make up our contemporary world. We have obviously come a long way since the invention of cinema at the end of the nineteenth century, let alone printing in the fifteenth. But it is important to remember that not all of the world has shared equally in these remarkable developments.

VIEWPOINT

'Today the globe has shrunk in the wash with speeded-up information from all directions. We have come, as it were, to live in a global village.'
Marshall McLuhan, inventor of the concept of the 'global village'.

DEBATE

Do more media mean better media? Does the existence of modern mass media such as television, video and DVD mean that we're wiser today than our ancestors were?

MEDIA OWNERSHIP

Public Educators, or Power-Crazed Tycoons?

William Randolph Hearst was keenly aware of the power that newspaper ownership could bring.

Why should we care who owns the media, as long as they provide us with what we want? We should care, because what the media produce can affect the health of democratic societies.

The media are not like those industries that produce things, such as cars, food and drinks. Although the media do produce objects such as books, magazines, CDs and DVDs, we buy these things for what is actually in or on them. In one way or another, they contain various kinds of knowledge and information that are important ingredients in the shaping of the culture to which we belong. That's why some people refer to the media as the 'consciousness industry' – because what they produce helps to form not only our consciousness of who we are but also our perceptions of our society and of the wider world in which we live.

It is because the media play this key social role that some people are worried that those who own them may use them for their own ends. This is of particular concern if media owners have a large number of different businesses. They are thus able, in principle at least, to spread their views across a wide range of media, reaching a huge number of people in the process.

In the centuries following the invention of printing, the authorities fully understood the power and importance of the printed media. That is why they tried to control them, usually by allowing only those of whom they approved to print books and other material. Often printers had to be licensed, and unlicensed printers could face imprisonment. During the nineteenth century, however, the written word began to escape from some of the more extreme forms of control by church and state. But, at the same time, publishing became an increasingly commercial business, and there were those for whom producing a newspaper became more a matter of turning a profit than informing the public. Thus, in a sense, the printed word escaped from one set of restrictions only to find itself ensnared by others. Nowhere was this clearer than in the case of the newspaper and the rise of the so-called 'press baron'.

The most notorious press baron was an American: William Randolph Hearst. He was the basis of *Citizen Kane* – a famous and controversial film about a ruthless newspaper tycoon. The reason why the power of the media owner is a cause for concern is neatly illustrated by the following true story.

VIEWPOINTS

'Independence from party, which had been sporadically claimed but never meaningfully realized, has become the norm among Britain's national newspapers.'
Stephen Koss. Professor of History at Columbia University, in The Rise and Fall of the Political Press in Britain

'I think it would be very unlikely that I would have a newspaper that would support the socialist party. That isn't what some people would call press freedom, but why should I want a product I didn't approve of? I believe it is in the best interests of United Newspapers in terms of its profits and shareholders to support the Conservatives.'
Lord Stevens. former owner of the Express group of newspapers.

Orson Welles as Charles Foster Kane in his classic 1941 film Citizen Kane. *Welles based his central character on the real life press baron William Randolph Hearst, who tried unsuccessfully to have the film suppressed.*

In 1898, immediately prior to the outbreak of the Spanish-American war in Cuba, the *New York Journal*'s artist, Frederic Remington, wired Hearst, the paper's owner, stating that: 'There is no trouble here. There will be no war. Wish to return'. Hearst swiftly replied: 'Please remain. You furnish the pictures, and I'll furnish the war'. His papers duly played their part in whipping-up pro-war feeling by running anti-Spanish articles, and the conflict soon followed.

In a similar vein, in Britain the press barons Lords Rothermere and Beaverbrook became convinced in the 1920s that the country's economic problems could be solved by making the British empire a free trade zone protected by high tariffs. They used their papers remorselessly to promote this scheme and, when they were unable to convince the Conservative leadership to support it, they turned their normally Conservative-supporting newspapers against the party and helped to found a new one, the United Empire Party. They then backed this party vociferously in their own pages in two London by-elections!

Fleet Street in 1921, with the Daily Mail office in the foreground. This was the street in which most of Britain's national papers were produced until the 1980s.

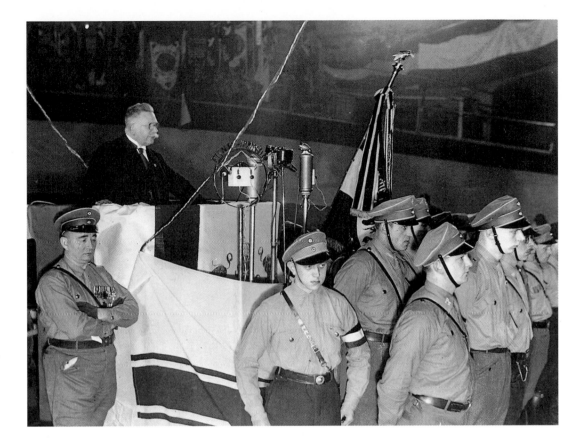

The press barons were not confined to North America and Britain. In 1920s Germany the industrialist Alfred Hugenberg built up formidable newspaper holdings, owning in Berlin alone the mass circulation *Lokal-Anzeiger*, *Berliner Nachtausgabe* and *Der Montag*, as well as fourteen provincial newspapers in cities such as Munich and Stuttgart. But these papers were only one part of his vast media empire, which also included book publishing and Germany's largest film studio, Ufa. In the late 1920s and early 1930s, Hugenberg swung all these behind the right-wing political party of which he was chairman and which helped the Nazis to power. Hugenberg's ownership of so many different kinds of media foreshadowed today's vast, global, multi-media conglomerates such as Time Warner, News International and Fininvest.

Right-wing politician, industrialist and media magnate Alfred Hugenberg speaking at a meeting of the German National People's Party in February 1933, just before the Nazis seized power in Germany.

VIEWPOINT

'Every extension of the franchise renders more powerful the newspaper and less powerful the politician.'
Alfred Harmsworth, later to become Lord Northcliffe, proprietor of the Daily Mail, The Times and London Evening News, in 1903.

VIEWPOINTS

'We need a more open, less monolithic system of broadcasting.'
An editorial attacking the BBC, which appeared in The Times *(proprietor Rupert Murdoch) on 15 January 1985.*

'Monopoly is a terrible thing, until you have it.'
Rupert Murdoch, a few years later.

The model of a modern media magnate, Rupert Murdoch, whose numerous and diverse media interests stretch all around the globe.

Murdoch and News International

News International's interests include over 130 newspapers (mainly in Australia, Britain and the US), the Twentieth Century Fox film studio, the US Fox broadcasting network, Fox News Channel, the book publishers HarperCollins, the Asian satellite service Star Television, a controlling stake in the satellite service British Sky Broadcasting (BSkyB), and much more besides.

The company is owned by Rupert Murdoch, who has come to symbolize, for many, the dangers of too many media in the hands of one person or group. In particular, Murdoch has been accused of using his media, in the different countries in which he has commercial interests, to support those political parties with which he feels he can do business, and to undermine and attack parties whose policies are unfavourable towards him. He has also been charged with using his papers to hype his own film and TV productions and to attack his media rivals.

Currently, Murdoch is attempting to expand his media interests into the potentially vast and largely untapped Chinese market. This again has led to the criticism that, in attempting to woo the Chinese leaders, he has put his own financial concerns before the interests of media freedom. When BBC World Service Television displeased the Chinese government by its critical coverage of the treatment of human rights protestors in China, Murdoch threw the BBC off the Star service as soon as he acquired it. He also refused to allow HarperCollins to publish the memoirs of Chris Patten, the last governor of Hong Kong, because they painted an unflattering picture of the Chinese leaders.

Media coverage of the 1989 demonstrations in Peking's Tiananmen Square, and the eventual suppression of these demonstrations by the authorities, helped to bring home to the world China's poor human rights record.

Politics and power

It is clearly dangerous for the media to become increasingly concentrated in fewer and fewer hands – and Murdoch is not the only latter-day example illustrating this. In Italy, media magnate Silvio Berlusconi runs a company called Fininvest, which owns an advertising agency, the country's largest book and magazine publisher, the football club A C Milan, and the three main commercial TV channels (among much else).

FACT

In 1995, the United States enjoyed a trade surplus (in other words, it exported far more than it imported) with Europe in media products of all kinds of $6.3 billion, more than triple the size of its surplus in 1988. Media exports play a key role in the US economy, surpassed only by the country's aerospace industry.

In Italy during the 1990s, Silvio Berlusconi (right) used his media empire, and especially his television stations, to launch his own political movement, Forza Italia.

Berlusconi used his media interests to create a political party Forza Italia (named after a football chant, which translates roughly as 'Come on, Italy!'). He went on to propagandize very successfully on its behalf – so much so, that in the 1994 Italian elections he himself became prime minister at the head of a coalition government in which his party occupied a key role! On coming to power, one of his first acts was to try to weaken the power of the public broadcaster RAI – his main rival for television audiences.

Maintaining diversity

It could be argued that the instances of media barons using their empires to further their own interests are exceptions. There are huge groups such as Time Warner, Disney, Bertelsmann, Sony, Polygram, Universal and NBC, which use their media rather more responsibly, and in a less self-interested fashion. This may be the case, but it doesn't get round the fact that too many media in too few hands poses at least a potential threat to the diversity, or variety, of information of one kind or another. And this diversity ought to be the hallmark of a democratic society. That is why most democratic societies place limits on the amount of media that one person or group may own. Furthermore, some countries believe their media to be of such national importance that they won't allow foreigners to own them. This is why Rupert Murdoch had to shed his Australian nationality and take on American citizenship when he wanted to buy Twentieth Century Fox!

As ownership of the media becomes concentrated in the hands of fewer and fewer powerful people, the debate about the consequences – and in particular the threat to the variety, reliability and objectivity of the information put out by the media – looks set to run and run.

VIEWPOINTS

'[Broadcasting is] a public service whose prime responsibility is to develop the cultural rights of modern citizenship.'
Graham Murdock, in Behind the Screens: the Structure of British Television in the Nineties.

'Television is just another appliance. It's a toaster with pictures.'
Mark Fowler, President Reagan's first appointee as head of the Federal Communications Commission (the main regulator of the American media industries).

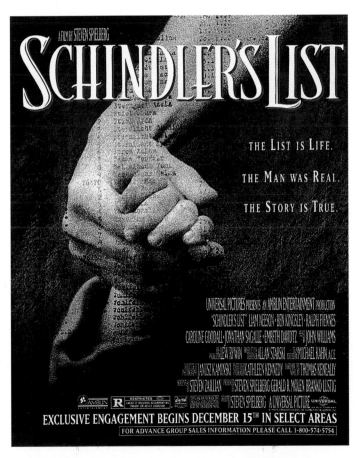

A poster for Schindler's List – a Hollywood film about the experiences of Jewish people in concentration camps during the Second World War. Films such as this show that commercial media can perform a valuable social and educational role and are not profit-oriented to the exclusion of all other considerations.

DEBATE

Should individuals be banned from owning huge media corporations?

REGULATING THE MEDIA

A Guiding Hand, or a Governing Body?

We tend to think of uncensored media as one of the defining characteristics of a democratic society, with censored media as one of the marks of a non-democratic one. But many people, in Western Europe at least, have traditionally believed that the broadcast media play too important a role in society to be left simply to their own devices and to the mercy of market forces. Such people have argued that broadcasting needs to be regulated, or controlled, in the interests of society as a whole. By comparison, the press has largely been regarded as the private property of its owners, theirs to do with what they will, provided their papers obey the laws of the land in matters concerning defamation, obscenity, national security and so on.

Not all media regulation is a form of censorship, or suppression. For example, the media may be regulated to ensure that they reflect a wide range of views and that they are owned by a variety of different people. There may be public subsidies, or grants (as in France) to small media concerns that might otherwise be overwhelmed in the marketplace by large ones. In most countries in the European Union, the law allows a statutory right of reply to those who have been seriously misrepresented by the media. Such measures may be seen as positive forms of regulation, rather than negative forms of censorship. Perhaps the best example of this kind of positive regulation is shown by the way in which public service broadcasting has traditionally operated in Europe.

For many, BBC Television's adaptation of the Jane Austen novel, Pride and Prejudice, *symbolizes the kind of quality programme that only public service broadcasting is able and willing to produce.*

Public service broadcasting

Western European countries, unlike the United States, have always avoided wholly commercial broadcasting. Equally, and unlike the Eastern European countries once under Soviet domination, they have also steered clear of the state-controlled model. Instead, they have tended to opt for an 'arm's length' relationship between broadcasters and the state. In this relationship, the broadcasters are regulated not by the government of the day, but by people who are chosen to represent the public interest. In Britain, for example, a public corporation such as the BBC is regulated by the Board of Governors. Private companies, such as Channel 4 and the ITV franchise holders (those television companies granted a licence to broadcast on the ITV network), are regulated by the members of the Independent Television Commission (ITC). The latter is a publicly funded body responsible for licensing and regulating commercially funded television services.

FACT

Twenty-five countries around the world imprison journalists for offences connected with their profession. In 1999, about 100 journalists were behind bars.

Governments themselves do not draw up the regulations governing broadcasting. Instead they detail the broad principles under which broadcasting should operate and leave it to those representing the public interest within the broadcasting system to draft the appropriate codes of practice.

The way in which this is done varies from one European country to another, as does the method of financing, which may involve some form of licence fee, subscription or advertising revenue, or a mixture of all three. But it is possible to identify the general principles under which public service broadcasting, as it is called, has traditionally operated in Europe. These are:

- broadcasting services should be able to be received by everybody, regardless of where they live
- programmes should cater for all interests and tastes, including minority ones
- broadcasters should recognize their medium's role in helping to sustain a sense of national identity and cultural community
- broadcasting should distance itself from all vested interests, and especially those of the government of the day
- the purpose of broadcasting must be the making of quality programmes at all levels which are good in themselves and not intended merely to maximise audience numbers.

Government bias?

Of course, it could be argued that public service broadcasters all too often fail to live up to these high ideals, or that their 'arm's length' relationship with the state still results in censorship of one kind or another. Thus, in Italy up until the 1970s, the public broadcaster RAI was generally regarded as the embodiment of the voice of the ruling

Christian Democratic Party. In France, prior to the broadcasting reforms introduced by President Mitterand in the 1980s, governments tended to regard television and radio as 'theirs'. Therefore every time a new government was elected, the entire senior management staff of the broadcasting system was replaced. Such political interference meant that in the 1960s French broadcasters were unable to cover the war in Algeria properly.

Meanwhile, in Britain, news coverage of the Irish 'troubles' has been the subject of close scrutiny. The troubles revolve around the British government's attempts to deal with the difficult fact that one part of the population of Northern Ireland wishes to remain part of the United Kingdom whilst another wants reunification with the Republic of Ireland. Successive governments have tended to regard any attempt to deal with this subject in a manner that does not absolutely reflect the government line as equal to treason.

French media coverage of the Algerian War of Independence (1954-62) was subject to strict censorship, and television coverage was particularly restricted.

Sinn Fein president, Gerry Adams. Sinn Fein was one of the political parties which found its access to the British media severely restricted by a broadcasting ban imposed by the British government in 1988. The ban was not lifted until 1994.

This approach has led to the BBC being pressured (successfully) to ban an episode of the 'Real Lives' series entitled *Edge of the Union*, which it was felt gave too much uncontested space to 'extremists' from both sides of the divide. The Independent Broadcasting Authority (the predecessor of the ITC) was leaned on (unsuccessfully) to ban *Death on the Rock*, a programme which questioned the 'official version' of an SAS ambush and killing of suspected IRA terrorists in Gibraltar. And, in 1988, a ban was imposed by the Conservative government of the day, led by Prime Minister Margaret Thatcher, on broadcast interviews with and statements by a whole number of Irish organizations.

So, a broadcasting system regulated according to public service principles has its downside too, and positive obligations can all too easily shade off into negative prohibitions. But we should also remember that wholly commercial media are also regulated – though in less obvious ways. We have already seen in the previous chapter how media owners can act as censors. It is important to bear in mind that market forces and the dictates of the 'bottom line' – in other words, money – effectively regulate the commercial media.

Channel flannel

Commercial broadcasting is funded largely, or in some cases solely, by advertising. There's nothing necessarily wrong in this of course. But this system ultimately rests on selling audiences to advertisers, and not programmes to audiences. Television companies do their best to woo advertisers, and this puts a great deal of potential power over programming in the hands of the advertisers. In the United States the advertisers are so powerful that they have in many cases effectively become the programmes' 'sponsors'. At worst, this can seriously discriminate against programming which doesn't attract really big audiences, or a smaller audience of big spenders, and may discourage the production of programmes which might in some way offend those who are, in effect, footing the bill. This is the kind of broadcasting which, it is often alleged, threatens to clog up the airwaves with 'satellite slush' and 'channel flannel'.

As Grant Tinker, a former head of NBC-TV observed, US television 'is an advertising supported medium, and to the extent that support falls out, programming will change'. And support can, and indeed does, 'fall out' when advertisers don't like a programme's point of view.

In the US, a scandal of the 1950s involved a TV game show called Twenty-One. The show was revealed to have been rigged by its producers to satisfy the wishes of the sponsors. Here one of the contestants, Charles van Doren, pretends to consider a question to which he has already been given the answer.

In a more general sense, advertisers tend not to like programmes that interfere with the 'buying mood'. This attitude reduces the television schedule to the level of a suitable environment for the selling of goods and services, and squeezes out 'difficult', disturbing or demanding programmes.

American television is often held up as a dire warning in this respect. But it is actually no worse than many of the purely commercial channels that have sprung up in Europe since the public service broadcasters lost their monopolies. These channels – which include BSkyB in the UK and the Berlusconi channels in Italy – are often heavily reliant on programmes imported from the United States. On the other hand, the Public Broadcasting Service (PBS) in the US imports a good deal of material from British public service broadcasters. However, although extremely popular with certain sections of the population, PBS has never been a strong institution financially, and has found itself under increasing attack from conservatives opposed to even the slightest federal funding for broadcasting.

Legal restrictions

In this chapter we've looked at the different ways in which broadcasting can be regulated in democratic societies. In such societies, broadcasters, along with those in the other media, also have to obey the laws of the land in matters such as libel, official secrecy, confidentiality, obscenity, incitement to violence and racial hatred, and so on. How these laws operate varies widely from one democratic society to another. And, while such laws are made supposedly in the public interest, they can also constitute a formidable regulatory obstacle in the path of freedom of expression.

Finally, there are still countries in the world today in which the media are controlled directly and totally by the state. The all-too-long roll call includes Afghanistan, North Korea, Saudi Arabia, Iraq, Iran, Serbia, Ethiopia and Cuba. In countries such as these, the media as we know them barely exist. In so far as they do, they are extremely limited in both number and in what they are permitted to print or broadcast, being regarded by the authorities as simply the voice of the state. While citizens of democratic countries may disagree with the ways in which the media are regulated within their own societies – whether by market forces, statute law, committees of experts, or by a combination of these – it is worth remembering that media regulation could be much more extreme.

DEBATE

Can media regulation actually improve media freedom?

In Kabul, Afghanistan, the Taliban militia has imposed strict laws in the areas under its control. These laws include the banning of music and television. Here militia members burn movie film outside a cinema.

THE MEDIA AND PROPAGANDA

Mass Communication, or Mass Indoctrination?

When people encounter in the media political ideas with which they disagree, they often accuse the media of spreading propaganda. But this knee-jerk use of the term doesn't tell us anything about what propaganda actually is. Propaganda is the deliberate use of newspapers, television and other media to influence people's attitudes, often employing lies and distortion. The use of the word 'propaganda' can be traced back to the seventeenth century, when Pope Gregory XV set up the missionary organization, the *Congregatio de Propaganda Fide* (Congregation for the Propagation of the Faith), to counteract the ideas of the Protestant Reformation. In the eighteenth and nineteenth centuries the word was used in a more or less neutral sense in most European countries to refer to the spreading of political and religious beliefs, and also to commercial advertising.

The totalitarian model
It was really in the twentieth century that propaganda took on the negative connotations that we are familiar with today. This was mainly the result of two societies that made the most widespread and deliberate use of the media for propaganda purposes. These were the Soviet Union and Nazi Germany.

In the Soviet Union, the communist leader Vladimir Ilyich Lenin argued that the newspaper should be a 'collective propagandist, collective

Propaganda films made under Nazi rule included Leni Riefenstahl's Olympische Spiele, *a record of the 1936 Olympic Games. In this film images of the human body were used to celebrate the health and strength of a supposedly reinvigorated Germany.*

agitator, collective organizer'. He also argued that the cinema 'must be directed to a single unitary goal – the struggle for the new life, for new customs, for a better future, for the blossoming of science and art'. From 1917 up until the 1980s, the Soviet authorities used the media remorselessly to propagandize on behalf of communist values and to persuade people that what was known as 'actually existing socialism' represented some kind of earthly paradise for working people. In Nazi Germany, between 1933 and 1945, the media endlessly extolled the vision of the Thousand Year Reich, a proud and powerful new Germany arisen from the humiliations of the First World War. The Reich promised a Germany purged of 'foreign' elements such as communism, socialism, democracy and of those groups of people believed to be ethnically 'impure', in particular the Jews.

What took place under communist rule in the Soviet Union and under Nazi rule in Germany was the systematic and deliberate use of the media by a political party and the state. These agencies ruthlessly controlled the media to spread a particular ideology, or set of ideas. It was a conscious and co-ordinated attempt to use the media to try and make people view the world in a particular light and from a particular political angle. And this is a workable definition of what political propaganda, in its purest and most developed form, actually is and does. However, the use of propaganda by these regimes was by no means confined only to the media; every social institution, including the schools, universities and even the family, was expected to play its part in spreading the ideological message.

Censorship today

It would be comforting, but mistaken, to think that this process of political propaganda is safely consigned to the history books. However, as mentioned in the preceding chapter, there are still many countries in the world whose governments censor the media, and these are equally prone to use the media under their control for propaganda purposes too. For example, in February 1989 the Ayatollah Khomeini of Iran used Tehran radio to broadcast his infamous *fatwa* (religious edict) on the author Salman Rushdie. This effectively called on Muslims to kill Rushdie for his book, *The Satanic Verses*.

In India, Muslims demonstrate against the publication of Salman Rushdie's novel, The Satanic Verses, *which they claimed blasphemed their faith.*

Long before the first shots were fired in the wars between the republics of the former Yugoslavia during the 1990s, the governments of those republics had been using the media at their disposal to play on people's fears of and prejudices about ethnic and religious differences. They thus paved the way for the bloody disintegration that inevitably followed.

The democratic model

On the other hand, propaganda, like censorship, is not confined to undemocratic societies. For example, during the Second World War, both the British and American media engaged in strenuous propaganda on behalf of the war effort. In Britain a Ministry of Information was formed whose function it was to 'present the national case to the public at home and abroad', and to this end it was responsible for the 'preparation and issue of National Propaganda'. The media, and especially the cinema, were tasked with the making of morale-boosting products, from jolly radio programmes such as *Music While You Work* and *Workers' Playtime* through to newsreels, short films and feature films. The reporting in the press and on the radio of military defeats and of other depressing events was actively discouraged and, on occasion, expressly forbidden.

In the United States, the film industry had begun to produce anti-Nazi films such as *Confessions of a Nazi Spy* and certain episodes of the *March of Time* newsreels even before the country entered the war in late 1941. In 1942 President Roosevelt actually classified Hollywood as 'an essential war industry'. Hollywood played a crucial role in explaining to the American people, in an entertaining as well as informative way, why they were fighting in what might otherwise have been regarded as a European war.

VIEWPOINTS

'The receptive powers of the masses are very restricted, and their understanding is feeble. On the other hand, they quickly forget. Such being the case, all effective propaganda must be confined to a few bare essentials and those must be expressed as far as possible in stereotyped formulae.'
Adolf Hitler, in Mein Kampf, *1925.*

'The best propaganda is not that which is always openly revealing itself; the best propaganda is that which as it were works invisibly, penetrates the whole of life without the public having any knowledge at all of the propagandist initiative.'
Joseph Goebbels, Reichsminister for Propaganda, Germany 1933-45.

After the Japanese attack on Pearl Harbor, the American public was bombarded with propaganda on behalf of the war effort. The Office of War Information distributed its major posters in runs of 1.5 million, and the Army Signal Corps produced 3,000 films that eventually reached over 8.5 million viewers a month. In an average week in American cinemas, 50 million viewers watched official information films (short films that generally preceded the main feature film), and by 1943 nearly one third of Hollywood movies had a war theme. The US War Department spent more than $50 million annually on film production during the war.

With men away fighting, women were needed to join the US work force during the Second World War. A great deal of propaganda was aimed at encouraging women to take up what had previously been regarded as men's jobs.

To most people, this would appear as entirely unsurprising, and probably admirable. Who, after all, would not have wanted the media to play their part in defeating an enemy such as Nazi Germany? But should there be a propaganda role for the media in peacetime in democratic societies? Most people would probably answer 'no'. But, then, what about party political broadcasts, or government campaigns conducted via the media that warn against the dangers of contracting AIDS or of drink driving, or that encourage people to join literacy schemes? Are these examples of a type of propaganda that actively helps society? Or are they just the superficially nicer face of the forces of state control?

Matters become even more complicated when we look at what happens when democratic countries become involved in wars that, unlike the two global conflicts of the twentieth century, don't actually threaten their very existence. For example, during the Falklands War between Britain and Argentina in 1982, the 1990-91 Gulf War between Iraq and United Nations forces (which included substantial contingents from the United States and United Kingdom), and in the recent NATO action against Serbia over Kosovo, the media in the western countries involved became active propagandists for the war effort. Should they have done so, on the grounds that troops from their countries were active participants? Or should they have remained neutral, on the grounds that many people in these countries were actually opposed to these conflicts and deserved, in a democracy, to have their voices heard? Such questions take on an added significance when asked in the light of an earlier, and equally controversial, conflict, namely the Vietnam War. During this war (1964-75), American media coverage was blamed, rightly or wrongly, for igniting public opposition to the conflict and making the war effectively unwinnable.

> ## FACT
>
> In Saudi Arabia the Ministry of Information approves the hiring of editors and can dismiss them at will. Criticism of the Saudi royal family and reporting on sensitive political topics are forbidden. The state closely monitors, and where it feels it necessary, censors, all foreign publications entering the country.

Positive media images of British troops in Kosovo during the 1999 Balkan War were a far cry from much media coverage of the Vietnam War.

Depending on your point of view...

Controversies about the media and propaganda are by no means confined to wartime. Those who criticize the media in democratic societies for routinely acting as propagandists fall, broadly speaking, into two camps. Conservatives often see the media as a 'liberal conspiracy', while radicals attack it for propping up the system and the status quo. In the United States the conservatives' target tends to be the press, while the radicals reserve most of their wrath for television and radio. Radicals argue that talk shows of the kind hosted by Howard Stern and other 'shock jocks', and stations run by Christian fundamentalists, peddle ideas which, though perhaps not always appearing to be overtly 'political', fit in with the world-view of the hard-line Republican right. In Britain, it is precisely the other way round. Public

US 'shock jock' Howard Stern deliberately courts controversy in the media.

service broadcasting has long been regarded as overly liberal by many conservatives, while radicals have complained that most of the daily press consists of undiluted propaganda for the Conservative Party.

It could be argued that the different sets of views in the different media neatly balance each other out. On the other hand, perhaps the citizens of democratic societies would be better served if all of their media were balanced and impartial, and not propagandists for one viewpoint or another. But would this make for deadly dull media that few would want to watch, listen to or read? And, even if impartiality is thought to be desirable, is it ever actually achievable in practice?

Finally, some radicals suggest that the 'liberal' media are considerably less liberal than the conservatives suppose! They argue that in all democratic societies the media tend increasingly to operate with a narrow, restricted set of views about society and the world at large. They also argue that the media depend ever more heavily and uncritically on various official and corporate sources of information. According to such theorists, the media are so deeply locked into the market system that they are businesses first and foremost. This means that the profit motive is more important than any informative function they are supposed to have. This applies particularly to those media, such as newspapers and magazines, that rely for their survival on advertising.

This approach has been criticized as being far too sweeping, and as portraying the media as part of some giant conspiracy by 'the powers that be'. It fails to take account of the fact that the media have played a key role, from time to time, in exposing political and corporate corruption. (The most famous example of this is the Watergate scandal, in which journalists on the *Washington Post* revealed that members of President Nixon's administration had illegally tapped the phones of his political opponents.) On the other hand, the critical approach raises interesting questions – such as how do the media get the information that they then pass on to us? Are the media part of the 'system', or a watchdog over it? And what are the consequences of the media being enmeshed in 'big business'?

VIEWPOINTS

'Money and power are able to filter out the news fit to print, marginalize dissent, and allow the government and dominant private interests to get their messages across to the public'
Noam Chomsky and Edward Herman outlining their 'propaganda model' of the media. Chomsky is one of America's foremost social critics and Institute Professor in the Department of Linguistics and Philosophy at the Massachusetts Institute of Technology.

'To me, Berlusconi is eternal.... I love Silvio Berlusconi.'
Emilio Fede presenting the news during the 1994 Italian elections, which were won by Berlusconi's Forza Italia party. He was speaking on Italy's Rete 4, which is owned by... Silvio Berlusconi.

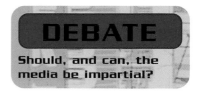

DEBATE

Should, and can, the media be impartial?

ADVERTISING, AND HOW IT WORKS

Financial Lifeline, or Hidden Persuader?

The luxury goods sector makes just as much use of advertising as does the mass-market sector, as this 1910 Italian poster of a woman wearing a fur stole demonstrates.

Except in the form of leaflets, posters and hoardings (large boards used for displaying posters), advertising is not a medium in itself. Instead, advertisers use the various media to put across their messages. Without the revenue generated by advertising, commercial television would not exist, and newspapers and magazines would be far too expensive for most people to buy, so many of them would probably vanish from view.

Advertising-funded media

By the end of the nineteenth century, in both America and Europe, mass circulation newspapers and magazines had already become heavily dependent on advertising for their continued existence. Also the producers of goods and services had begun to allocate a significant proportion of their income to advertising. In the United States, for example, spending on advertising rose from $15 million in 1870 to $39 million in 1880, and to $71 million in 1890. By 1908, spending had reached over $140 million, with most of this going to newspapers and, increasingly, magazines. The growth of illustrated magazines in the late nineteenth century, in both the United States and Europe, demonstrated that cheap, high circulation, advertising-funded media could be economically viable. This not only set an example to the developing popular newspaper press, but also laid the groundwork for all subsequent developments in the commercialization of the media.

At first, producers paid the media directly to carry their advertisements. Then, in the middle of the nineteenth century, advertising agencies began to be created, and these companies charged producers for placing their advertisements in the appropriate media. The first independent agency in North America was set up by Volney Palmer in Philadelphia in 1842. By the 1860s, the steadily growing number of agencies had begun offering to design and produce the advertisements as well. By the end of the century they were organizing advertising campaigns either in one particular medium or, as became increasingly the case, across a whole range of media. The agencies thus became vast media businesses in their own right.

Matching audience with product

Even before the end of the nineteenth century, publishers had begun to regard their publications not so much as products to be sold to readers, but more as a way of organizing audiences into clearly identifiable target groups such as sports fans, theatregoers, women interested in fashion, women interested in cooking, and so on. These readership groups could then be sold to advertisers. The audiences themselves became the 'products' generated by the media industry. This selling of audiences to advertisers was to become a highly refined media marketing strategy, especially with the development of radio and television.

Advertisements perform an important function by promoting brand loyalty. Here humour is used to encourage New Zealanders to choose a particular brand of scourer.

The enormous growth of advertising has worried many people. It has been accused of being a 'hidden persuader', manipulating and influencing consumers without their being fully aware of it. It has been charged with creating 'false needs', in other words with making us want things that are not necessary for our survival but play on desires such as 'keeping up with the Joneses'. Some argue that advertising presents us with seductive but ultimately unrealistic images of people and lifestyles, which make us discontented and unhappy when we inevitably fail to live up to them. And even if it is admitted that advertising isn't always successful at selling individual products and services, it is accused of all too effectively 'selling' values that encourage a high rate of spending and consumption, and of promoting products that are harmful, such as tobacco.

Brand loyalty

In response, the defenders of advertising argue that it isn't as powerful as is often supposed. Our own experience tells us that we do not automatically buy, or even want to buy, everything we see advertised, and that advertising cannot make people do anything they didn't want to do in the first place. All advertising does, according to the advertiser, is to try to alter the detail of the shopper's behaviour. It does this by encouraging people to prefer one brand to another by making it seem more attractive – hence the enormous effort that now goes into tailoring all sorts of products and services to people's 'life-styles', be they sun-dried tomatoes, pension plans or specialist holidays. The defenders are quick to point out that advertising does not achieve this on its own, but that it is just one element of a much wider marketing campaign.

From a different angle, advertising is accused of exercising too much power over the media it funds.

At worst, advertisers can act, or try to act, as censors. For example, NBC dropped the environmental series *In Which We Live* because sponsors were put off by its suggestions that corporate interests were at least partly responsible for environmental problems. And none of the major American networks would screen the hugely successful British comedy series *Absolutely Fabulous* because sponsors did not want to be associated with such risqué subject matter.

Less dramatically, the media that depend to a significant extent on advertising revenue may tailor their output to the advertisers' requirements. Hence the growth of life-style and leisure newspaper sections and supplements, whose main reason for being there is the advertising they attract. This trend is also witnessed in the growth of 'advertorials' – in other words, advertising masquerading as editorial text.

Modern marketing techniques promote the idea of certain kinds of 'lifestyles' into which the goods and services they are promoting can be seductively fitted. This advertisement was part of the new Jaguar S-Type launch campaign in 1999.

AS
FASHIONS
CHANGE,
STYLE
REMAINS.

The little black dress. The Schiaparelli gown. Beyond fashion, to enduring, immutable style. The warm sheen of polished maple. The perfect curve of a headlight. The classic sweep of a grille. The thrilling low growl of a powerful Jaguar engine. The spirited new Jaguar S-TYPE. Beyond fashion. Within reach. For information call 0800 70 80 60. www.jaguar.com

THE NEW JAGUAR S-TYPE.

JAGUAR
DON'T DREAM IT. DRIVE IT.

In a more general sense, the media has become increasingly obsessed with the numbers game – attracting the largest possible audiences in order to attract the most lucrative advertising. In the process, the media's role as anything other than a profitable business is often ignored – minority tastes are rejected in favour of majority ones, and the more challenging and demanding articles and programmes are sacrificed in favour of the bland and merely entertaining.

It is because funding the media by advertising has such negative consequences, the critics argue, that publicly funded organizations such as the BBC in the UK, RAI in Italy and PBS in the United States must continue to exist. On the other hand, defenders of advertising point out that, without it, many media that today we take for granted would simply cease to exist.

A great deal of creative effort and imagination, not to mention expense, goes into producing today's advertisements.

THE INFLUENCE OF THE MEDIA

Popular Entertainer, or Dangerous Role Model?

Ever since the invention of printing, some people have seen the media as a bad influence in one way or another. Long before the twentieth century, the printed media and other forms of popular entertainment were accused variously of spreading propaganda, whipping-up social unrest and lowering moral standards. In the twentieth century the stress was still predominantly on the negative, as opposed to the positive, influence of the media. The list of accusations levelled at the media has expanded to include the following vices:

- the promotion of consumerism
- the turning of television viewers into couch potatoes
- the contribution to a general process of 'dumbing down', or lowering cultural standards
- the encouragement of 'copycat' crimes
- the blurring in people's minds of the difference between images and reality.

Fears about the negative influence of the media have a long history in Britain. From various forms of music in the Cromwellian era, eighteenth-century popular theatre, nineteenth-century music hall, the cheap Victorian fiction known as 'penny dreadfuls' through to cinema and then television and video in our own time, the popular media have

The fact that many children watch a good deal of television has led to worries about the negative effects that it might be having on them.

always been accused by some as lowering morality and encouraging crime amongst the young. As George Orwell, the author of *Animal Farm* and *1984* once put it: 'the genuinely popular culture of England is something that goes on beneath the surface, unofficially and more or less frowned on by the authorities.' In short, the modern media have always been seen by some as a 'bad thing'.

The yellow press

Nor were such fears confined to Britain. In the United States, the 'yellow press', which we encountered in Chapter 1, was increasingly attacked as a bad influence at the start of the twentieth century. These papers frequently concentrated on the darker and more sensational aspects of modern life and, on the principle of shooting the messenger for bringing the bad news, were all too often blamed for actually causing the contemporary evils they reported. It's also hard to

Complaints about the media lowering moral standards are nothing new. In Britain this charge was levelled against the music hall, and in particular one of its greatest stars, the comedian Max Miller.

avoid the conclusion that because these publications were read by the young, the working class and the less well-educated they were perceived as all the more dangerous because their audience, so it was supposed, were naive, impressionable and open to suggestion.

Embarrassing and economically damaging cinema boycotts by the Legion of Decency, whose members are shown here in 1934, played a key role in forcing Hollywood to introduce strict self-censorship in the early 1930s.

Meanwhile, the cinema was also coming under fire as a source of negative influences. In 1909 the mayor of New York ordered the police to close every cinema in New York City, and by the early 1920s a significant number of states had introduced film censorship within their boundaries. This greatly alarmed the growing film industry, which introduced its own self-regulation in an attempt to hold off further action by individual states. However, in 1933, American Catholic bishops announced the formation of the Legion of Decency, an organization specifically designed not only to fight for what the Church considered to be 'better' films but also to organize boycotts of films it found offensive and dangerous.

VIEWPOINTS

'It should be cause for concern that, in the values and mores of modern society, we have created a quagmire from which monsters are bound to emerge.... Far too much of what passes for popular entertainment pollutes our society and creates a new tolerance in which what was thought to be beyond the pale becomes acceptable. Young minds are particularly vulnerable.'
Andrew Neil, former editor of The Sunday Times.

'Despite regular interest in effects, the pattern of findings across a broad range of issues has been disappointing. Evidence for direct influence is generally weak with many trivial results reported which are themselves controversial.... Theories abound, examples multiply, but convincing facts that specific media content is reliably associated with particular effects have proved quite elusive.'
Guy Cumberbatch and Dennis Howitt, in a study undertaken for the UK Broadcasting Standards Council.

Will H Hays, founder of the famous Hays Code, poses with a child.

After the Legion had organized a successful boycott of cinemas in Philadelphia, the industry took real fright and agreed to the much more rigorous enforcement of its own censorship code – known as the Hays Code after its founder Will H Hays. Among other things this laid down that 'no picture shall be produced which will lower the moral standards of those who see it. Hence the sympathy of the audience shall never be thrown to the side of crime, wrong-doing, evil or sin.'

Hypodermics and magic bullets

As indicated in the earlier 'list of vices', some people believe that the influence of the media is so strong that it actually makes people behave in certain ways – for example, to commit violent acts or become sexually active. Similarly, the chapter on propaganda introduced the idea that if the media are used for propagandist purposes they can actually shape and even change people's political views. This is sometimes called the 'media effects' approach. The media effects approach sees the media as not simply influencing but directly affecting us. It is also known as the 'hypodermic' or 'magic bullet' approach; this describes the way in which media messages are seen as a powerful serum directly injected into the mind.

The objections to this idea of an all-powerful media were discussed in the previous chapter on advertising. And we have also seen that regimes that utilize the media to spread propaganda make equal use of other social institutions as well. But it is worth noting that this notion of the media being all-powerful still seems to hold sway over many people's minds.

Copycat crimes

For example, in Britain in the early 1970s the film *A Clockwork Orange* (a futuristic fantasy about a violent adolescent gang) was widely blamed for causing a spate of what were called 'clockwork crimes'. In the 1980s the *Rambo* films, which concerned the increasingly fanciful adventures of an embittered Vietnam veteran, were blamed for the Hungerford massacre, in which an armed man ran amok in a provincial British town, killing sixteen people. And in the 1990s *Child's Play III*, about a doll that comes to life with murderous intent, was blamed for the murder of two-year-old James Bulger in Liverpool.

The director Stanley Kubrick withdrew his film, A Clockwork Orange, after it was blamed for sparking off a number of 'copycat crimes'. After Kubrick's death in 1999, the film was re-released.

Natural Born Killers

Meanwhile in the United States a number of crimes were laid at the door of the film *Natural Born Killers*, the story of two young lovers who attract a media circus in the course of a murderous rampage across the south-west of the country. The Internet and certain forms of rock music were blamed for inflaming the perpetrators of the Columbine high school massacre, in which two students went on a lethal rampage with guns and pipe bombs, resulting in twelve deaths. In each case, investigation of these charges revealed little firm evidence to support them. But many people continue to believe in 'media effects' of this kind, even when their own experiences would probably suggest that the media do not affect them in such a direct and dramatic fashion. Why might this be so?

In the mid-1990s, Natural Born Killers *gained almost as notorious a reputation as* A Clockwork Orange *had in the early 1970s.*

One reason may be the large number of studies that appear at first sight to 'prove' the link between watching violent images and committing violent acts. Another reason may be that the media are an easy scapegoat at a time of widespread fear about the apparent rise in violent crime. Such crimes increased, so the argument goes, in the twentieth century, which also saw the massive development of cinema and television, some of whose product contains violence. Therefore there must be a causal connection between the two. However, it could just as easily be argued that violence in the media simply reflects real-life violence, whose causes are many and various. Whatever the case, there are those who firmly believe it has been proved that the media have direct causal effects on behaviour, and there are those who argue that no such proof yet exists. Furthermore there are those who maintain that the matter cannot be proved one way or the other, because the whole approach is based on a misunderstanding of the relationship between the media and their audiences.

FACT

The British Board of Film Classification refused to pass Oliver Stone's 1994 film *Natural Born Killers* until it had investigated every case in which the film was accused of sparking off 'copycat' crimes. It found no evidence to support any of the allegations.

DEBATE

Do violent films and TV programmes encourage real life crime?

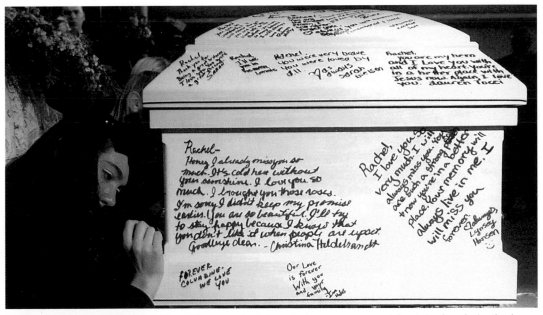

Rock music and the Internet were blamed by many for influencing the perpetrators of the Columbine high school massacre. Others blamed the tragedy on the easy availability of weaponry in the United States.

THE CONTROL OF KNOWLEDGE

A Window on the World, or a Distorting Mirror?

We have seen that the media are routinely blamed for directly causing a large number of social ills. While such charges, though frequently laid at the media's door, are not necessarily as well-founded as they might at first sight seem, this is by no means the same thing as saying that the media have no influence at all. After all, if they didn't, why would anyone want to work in the media? Why would anyone want to direct films, produce television programmes, or write in newspapers, magazines and books if they thought that it didn't make a blind bit of difference to their intended audience? And why would you be studying the media now if you didn't believe that they mattered in some way?

Journalists fight to photograph Princess Diana as she arrives in Lahore, India. Today, certain public figures are guaranteed to spark off a media 'feeding frenzy' wherever they go.

Shaping opinion

The media may not make us act or think in certain ways, but a moment's thought will tell us that we possess knowledge about, and attitudes towards, all sorts of people and events of which we have not the slightest first-hand experience. Where has all of this come from? Well, some of it may have come from parents, teachers and friends, but where have they got it from, if not at first-hand? It is here that the media in all their various forms must enter the picture. It is they who daily bring the wider world, be it distant parts of our own countries or far-flung parts of the globe, into our homes and our minds.

In western societies at least, television is the most important medium in this respect. More people watch television than read newspapers or listen to radio, and they generally trust television more than the other media as a reliable source of information. For example, the Independent Television Commission's publication *Television: the Public's View 1998* showed that television was the main source of world news for 71 per cent of respondents, as opposed to 14 per cent for newspapers and 8 per cent for radio. Indeed, even as a source of *local* news, television (40 per cent) scored over newspapers (38 per cent) and radio (9 per cent).

Public relations

Some people may think that this line of thinking makes the media, and especially television, seem more powerful than they actually are. After all, it could be argued, it is politicians and big business, at both national and international levels, who really set the agenda, while the media simply follow in their wake. There may be a good deal of truth in this, but we need to remember that, in this age of media manipulators (known as 'spin doctors') and public relations (PR) consultants, those in the

VIEWPOINTS

'It is sometimes argued that people simply make up their own minds and are not influenced very much by what they read or see. Our own view is that television cannot exclusively shape people's thoughts or actions. Nonetheless it has a profound effect because it has the power to tell people the order in which to think about events and issues.'
Glasgow University Media Group.

'Audiences do, in fact, interpret messages variously. They also may transform them to correspond with their individual experiences and tastes. But when they are confronted with a message incessantly repeated in all cultural conduits, issuing from the commanders of the social order, their capacities are overwhelmed.... '
Herbert Schiller. Professor Emeritus of Communication at the University of California. San Diego. in Culture Inc: the Corporate Takeover of Public Expression.

VIEWPOINT

'When a dog bites a man, that is not news, because it happens so often. But if a man bites a dog, that is news.'
John B Bogart, American journalist, 1918.

news are acutely conscious of what kinds of stories interest those who make the news. Accordingly those people working in 'spin' and PR feed news journalists with the 'right' kind of stories and information. Equally they go to some lengths to conceal stories in which the media might well be extremely interested but which their clients would rather were kept tightly under wraps!

In spite of British Prime Minister Tony Blair's insistence that his children be protected from media intrusion, the birth of his and Cherie Blair's new baby in 2000 inevitably became a 'media event'.

So, the media do not simply reflect reality but can to some extent actually create reality (in the sense of helping to structure what are taken to be the key issues of the day). However, they do not do this alone but achieve it by working together with other powerful institutions in society.

News values

So, is there a 'media view' of the world which then transfers itself to media audiences? Certainly, if you read the morning paper and watch the breakfast news on television or listen to it on the radio, the stories themselves are remarkably similar, even if the broadcast and newspaper journalists sometimes treat the stories very differently. Is this similarity because the news items reported are simply important in themselves? Or is it because they are important only within a common set of what have come to be called 'news values' or, in other words, what news organizations regard as 'newsworthy'?

VIEWPOINTS

'The fundamental obligation of the reporter is to the truth.'
Fergal Keane, BBC journalist.

'News may be true, but it is not the truth, and reporters and officials seldom see it the same way.'
James Reston, US journalist.

Those in power would prefer some stories to be kept under wraps. But in an age of voracious media even Bill Clinton, the President of the United States, could not conceal his affair with White House intern Monica Lewinsky.

Stories about well-known figures such as Madonna are always considered especially 'newsworthy' by the media.

VIEWPOINT

'Journalists speak of "the news" as if events select themselves. Further, they speak as if which is the "most significant" news story, and which "news angles" are most salient, are divinely inspired. Yet of the millions of events which occur every day in the world, only a tiny proportion ever become visible as "potential news stories"; and of this proportion, only a small fraction are actually produced as the day's news in the news media. It therefore seems inescapable that certain values are at work in the selection of certain events as being "newsworthy", even if this process is a largely unconscious, routine one.'
Stuart Hall, Professor of Sociology at the Open University, UK.

A great deal of work has been done on this question of news values and newsworthiness, and different researchers have generally concluded that events are newsworthy if they contain some or all of the following:

- conflict
- relevance to the audience's own lives and experiences
- immediacy
- human interest (especially characters with whom the audience can identify)
- unexpectedness
- reference to powerful and influential countries
- reference to well-known people (be they pop stars or politicians, footballers or royalty)
- negativity (bad news is good news)
- continuity with long-running stories.

Of course, these news values may be interpreted differently from one news medium and one news organization to another. But these basic ideas about what makes 'the news' are so deeply embedded in the professional cultures of the western news media that they are largely taken for granted by journalists themselves, as well as by audiences. These values constitute what have been called 'frames'; this means that they impose order on the millions of events taking place daily in the world and enable journalists to organize them into a series of events which make some kind of sense. This means that certain events are selected and others dropped, certain aspects of stories emphasized and others downplayed, events routinely presented in one way as opposed to another, and so on. All of this takes place largely automatically, and as a matter of daily journalistic routine.

It may well be that in the high-speed world of the news media, where time is always at a premium and deadlines are constantly looming, such means of coping with the vast amounts of information that endlessly pour in are to some extent unavoidable. At the same time, however, it isn't difficult to see how the media's news values can lead to the world being represented in ways which some might regard as distorted, or even biased, even if this distortion or bias is completely unintentional.

All too often, the world's poorest countries are largely ignored by the western media until dramatic conflict breaks out there, as in the case of Rwanda during the 1990s.

For example, where does the stress on powerful and influential countries and well-known people leave the developing world and ordinary people? Might not the accent on 'human interest' stories encourage a drift towards triviality and 'infotainment' (news stories dressed up as entertainment)? How can the concern with immediacy be reconciled with the need to explain the reasons behind events? Does a concentration on 'bad news' lead to an over-emphasis on the amount of crime and violence taking place in society today? Do certain important stories simply get left out altogether just because they don't 'fit'?

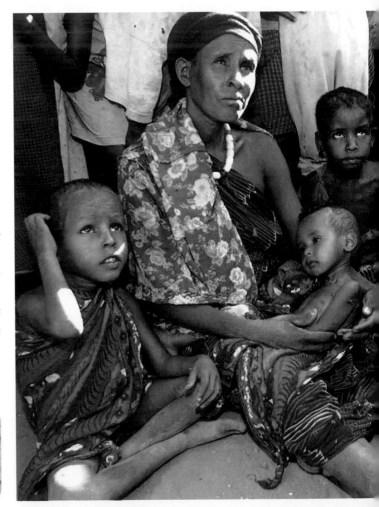

Heart-breaking and well-meaning pictures of famine victims, in this case in Ethiopia in 2000, may help to encourage much-needed relief efforts. But where is the other news about Ethiopia, not to mention its neighbours, in the western media?

DEBATE

Is journalism a window on the world, or a distorting mirror?

THE MEDIA IN THE INFORMATION SOCIETY

Into the Future, or Out of Control?

It is often said that we are living through an 'information revolution'. And, looking around us, it's obvious that there have been very considerable developments on the media front in recent years. Thanks to cable, satellite and digitalization it is now possible to receive a significantly increased number of television channels; more and more people are buying films on DVD as opposed to videocassette; and the home computer has become a familiar domestic object. As recently as thirty years ago, a computer with the capacity of even a modest contemporary desk-top model would have filled a whole room and would have been quite beyond the pockets of the ordinary person. Now, linked up to the Internet it is possible to have the world at your fingertips in a way that would have been unimaginable even a generation ago.

Smart technology

All of this has come about partly as an offshoot of research and development in what might at first sight appear to be areas entirely unrelated to the media – warfare and the exploration of space. Both of these areas require not only miniaturized (the development of things on a very small scale) but also extremely 'smart' (that is, computer-guided) technology. Also, as traditional 'heavy' manufacturing industries, such as steel-making and

The entertainment industries have played a major role in the development of virtual reality technologies. Here visitors get the chance to experience a virtual reality ride at Galbo amusement park in Japan.

coal-mining, declined across the western world, large corporations saw possibilities for investment and profit in the new electronic 'sunrise' industries, such as computer soft- and hardware production, and governments welcomed these as new sources of both employment and tax revenue. Furthermore, as the markets for 'white goods' (fridges, washing machines and the like) and televisions became saturated, consumer electronics companies began to search for new products and new markets. They also began to clamour to be let into the broadcasting and communications sectors which, in Western Europe at least, had always been the preserve of public enterprises. And finally, as companies became increasingly global, they needed ever more sophisticated means of communication in order to keep in touch with all the distant and different parts of their far-flung business empires.

Commercialization and convergence

The most dramatic consequences of these developments have been, firstly, the increasing commercialization of both broadcasting and telecommunications, which were previously treated as public services (again, in Western Europe) and, secondly, the increasing 'convergence' of those sectors. There is, today, a great deal of hype about the information revolution. It is almost impossible to open a newspaper or magazine without reading about the 'information superhighway' and the latest 'e-commerce' millionaires, or encountering numerous advertisements for the latest computer hardware and software. As these last all too clearly demonstrate, much of the hype is purely commercially driven – companies want you to buy, and keep on buying, their products! Of course, there's nothing necessarily wrong with this, and one cannot deny that the media, in their broadest sense, have undergone all sorts of important changes and developments in recent times. On the other hand, we need to bear in mind the continuities, as well as the breaks, with the rest of media history, and to understand that the questions raised by the latest developments in the media are much the same as those raised by previous ones.

One of the clearest signs of the information revolution is the presence of computers in schools and the high levels of computer literacy among many young people.

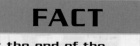

The recent merger between Time Warner and America Online has created a vast corporation straddling both 'old' and 'new' media. It is the most dramatic example yet of the 'merger mania' taking place in the communications field.

For example, a recent ruling in the United States could see the break-up of the multimedia giant Microsoft. This is on the grounds that it kept, in the words of Judge Thomas Jackson, an 'oppressive thumb' on the computer software market, supplying its Internet browser as a package with its Windows operating system, which is now used on over 90 per cent of the world's computers. The company thus used anti-competitive means to maintain a stranglehold over the PC industry. This judgement was based on precisely the same kind of worries about the power of media monopolies that we explored in chapter two, as is the concern expressed in some quarters about the merger of Time Warner and America Online. Similarly, worries about pornography and political propaganda on the Internet are to a large extent new versions of the old fears about media content which we looked at in chapter six. Meanwhile, the increasing commercialization of the Internet raises exactly the same issues as the commercialization of the traditional media, a topic referred to throughout this book.

The effect on our lives

So, perhaps we should conclude by forgetting all the hype about how our lives will never be the same again thanks to the wonders of new communications and information technology. Perhaps we should simply ask ourselves, in a level-headed way, what are the main issues raised by these changes in the media for the various key aspects of our daily lives:

* Shopping: will shopping via the television and computer mean the death of the high street and the supermarket? Will we venture out of our

FACT

At the end of the twentieth century, 37 per cent of adults in Britain had online access either at home or work. However, whilst 60 per cent of those aged 18-24 were online, only 36 per cent of 35-64 year olds and 8 per cent of over-65s had access.

homes even less? Will our streets become clogged with vans delivering all those goods ordered over the Internet?

- Television: do more channels mean better television – or just more television? Will we learn to live in the 'zap culture' in which we restlessly change channels every few minutes, or will we become unable to distinguish between the stories we are fed and reality? Will television continue to produce quality programmes, or will there be an increasing trend towards trivialization?

- Education: will all schools be able to afford the benefits of computers? Who will train the teachers to help the pupils to get the best out of them? Will computers increase our knowledge – or just the amount of information in the world?

- Politics: will we be able to vote via computer on matters of national or local importance? Or will closed-circuit video cameras, data banks and the like lead to a 'surveillance society'? Will our politicians become increasingly obsessed with image and 'spin' over substance and policy? Will the media end up as the only bridge to political awareness for the mass of the population? What are the implications for democracy?

VIEWPOINTS

'The network will draw us together, if that's what we choose, or let us scatter ourselves into a million mediated communities. Above all, and in countless new ways, the information highway will give us choices that can put us in touch with entertainment, information, and each other.'
Bill Gates, co-founder of the Microsoft corporation, in The Road Ahead, *1995.*

'It is only among the better off – households with $75,000 or more in annual income – that PCs had become routine, with a 60-75% penetration rate.... Even the experience of the most favourably endowed ones in the global political economy shows, therefore, that the level and character of access remained a function of entrenched income inequality.'
Dan Schiller, Cornering the Market in Cyberspace, *1997.*

Will the growth of e-commerce mean that we'll no longer need to go shopping, and that instead our shopping will come to us?

- Work: will those who work in declining traditional industries be retrained to work in the new, information-based ones? Will there be enough work for everybody? Will those in work need constantly to learn new information-handling skills?
- Society: will western countries be divided between the information-rich and the information-poor, the computer-literate and computer-illiterate? And will these divisions repeat themselves on the world scale, between the developed and developing countries?

The new media landscape

These are some of the key questions raised by the new technologies of communication and information, which are the basis of our increasingly 'converged' media landscape today. These down-to-earth issues may not seem terribly glamorous compared to the visions of a computer-based utopia with which we are tempted by some of the more enthusiastic supporters of the information revolution. But they will have to be faced if we are to make the best of the undoubted opportunities already being offered to us by these developments in the media world. And the questions about who owns, controls, regulates, funds, and, of course, consumes the media are as relevant today as they ever were – if not more so.

As we have seen, the twentieth-century experience of the media, for all the pleasures that they brought to millions of people across the globe, was not always a particularly happy one. Perhaps by learning more about the media – their past as well as their present – we might even help to dispel some of the more irrational fears that still seem to surround them in some quarters. At the same time, if we are to navigate successfully today's increasingly crowded media landscape we need to take a questioning

If older people are to keep up with the information revolution, those without computer skills will need proper training.

stance towards these 'cultural industries'. As much as at any time in their turbulent history, the media today play an ever-growing role in our societies. They create jobs, generate revenue and, above all, constantly provide us with the information of every conceivable kind that we need in order to conduct our daily lives as informed citizens of a democratic society.

One of the most important industries in the world today – the information industry – represented here by a busy television newsroom.

VIEWPOINTS

'Robust and sustainable economic progress, strong democracies, better solutions to global and local environmental challenges, improved health care, and – ultimately – a greater sense of shared stewardship of our small planet.'
US Vice President Al Gore in 1994 on the benefits of a Global Information Infrastructure.

'In a class-stratified, commercially oriented society like the United States, cannot the information highway have the effect of simply making it possible for the well-to-do to bypass any contact with the balance of society altogether?'
Robert McChesney. The Internet and US Communication Policy-Making in Historical and Critical Perspective. *1996.*

DEBATE

Do more data and more information mean more knowledge and greater wisdom?

GLOSSARY

censorship the deliberate and systematic suppression of expression.

circulation the numbers of copies sold of a newspaper or magazine.

coalition government a government made up of a number of different political parties.

conglomerate a large company formed by the take-over and merging of various other companies.

Conservatives in Britain, the name of the main right-wing political party, which is also known as the Tory Party. In more general terms it tends to refer to those opposed to change and modernity.

corporate concerning big business.

defamation an attack on a person's good reputation.

democratic refers to those countries whose governments consist of representatives freely elected by the adult population as a whole.

e-commerce buying and selling goods and services by electronic means, such as tele-shopping or web sites.

impartial fair, unbiased, balanced, objective.

information superhighway the totality of new forms of communication such as the Internet and the World Wide Web.

mass literacy refers to a condition in which the majority of people in a society can read and write.

monopoly the exclusive control by one person, company or group of a commodity or service.

North not simply the northern countries of the globe, but a term increasingly used to designate the richer and more powerful nations of the world.

pornography images and/or words intended to stimulate sexual arousal.

propagandize to spread a doctrine, such as a political ideology or religious belief, in a systematic and deliberate fashion.

radicals those in favour of rapid and fundamental political and social change.

regulate to lay down rules and requirements.

shock jocks radio personalities (mainly in the US) who specialize in expressing extreme and controversial views on matters of everyday concern.

South not simply the countries of the southern part of the globe, but a term increasingly used to designate the poorer and less influential countries of the world.

sponsors advertisers responsible for playing a leading role in the funding of a particular broadcast programme.

status quo the existing state of things.

systematic deliberate; done according to a conscious plan.

utopia an imaginary perfect place or state of things.

vested interest a personal interest, usually financial, in a particular issue or situation.

BOOKS TO READ

Agents of Power, J Herbert
Altschull, Longman, 1995
A global account of how the
news media actually work.

Censorship, Sue Curry
Jansen, Oxford, 1991
A challenging account of the
history of censorship in both
democratic and non-
democratic societies.

The Global Media, Edward S
Herman and Robert W
McChesney, Cassell, 1997
A critical look at who owns
what in today's media world,
and why it matters.

The Information Society,
David Lyon, Polity, 1988
A clear and readable account
of the main issues surrounding
this controversial topic.

**An Introduction to Digital
Media**, Tony Feldman,
Routledge, 1997
Just what it says it is, and
admirably clearly written.

Moving Experiences, David
Gauntlett, John Libbey, 1995
A cool-headed and critical
approach to the question of
media effects and influence.

Propaganda and Persuasion,
by Garth S Jowett and Victoria
O'Donnell, Sage, 1992
An examination of what
propaganda is, how it works
and the ways in which it has
developed over the centuries.

**Social Communication in
Advertising**, William Leiss,
Stephen Kline, Sut Jhally,
Routledge, 1990
An account of the growth of
advertising and the
controversies surrounding it.

We the Media, Don Hazen
and Julie Winokur (eds), The
New Press, New York, 1997

USEFUL
ADDRESSES

UK

The Advertising Standards Authority
2 Torrington Place
London
WC1E 7HW

Article 19
Lancaster House
33 Islington High Street
London
N1 9LH

British Broadcasting Corporation (BBC)
Broadcasting House
Portland Place
London
W1A 1AA

The Campaign for Press and Broadcasting Freedom
8 Cynthia Street
London
N1 9JF

Independent Television Commission
33 Foley Street
London
W1P 7LB

Index on Censorship
Lancaster House
33 Islington High Street
London
N1 9LH

The Press Complaints Commission
1 Salisbury Square
London
EC4 8AE

USA

Center for Media Literacy
4727 Wilshire Boulevard
Suite 403
Los Angeles
CA 900010

Committee to Protect Journalists
330 Seventh Avenue
12th Floor
New York,
NY 10001
(This is global in scope.)

Electronic Frontier Foundation
1550 Bryant Street
Suite 725
San Francisco
CA 94103

Fairness and Accuracy in Reporting (FAIR)
130 West 25th Street
New York
NY 10001

Media Education Foundation
26 Center Street
Northampton
MA 01060

Project Censored
Sonoma State University
801 E. Cotati Avenue
Rohnert Park
CA 94928

It is worth noting that Article 19 and Index on Censorship, though both based in the UK, are decidedly global in scope.

 INDEX